WHY DO THORNY DEVILS HAVE
TWO HEADS?

AND OTHER CURIOUS REPTILE ADAPTATIONS

BY PATRICIA FLETCHER

Gareth Stevens
PUBLISHING

Please visit our website, www.garethstevens.com. For a free color catalog of all our high-quality books, call toll free 1-800-542-2595 or fax 1-877-542-2596.

Cataloging-in-Publication Data

Names: Fletcher, Patricia.
Title: Why do thorny devils have two heads? And other curious reptile adaptations / Patricia Fletcher.
Description: New York : Gareth Stevens Publishing, 2018. | Series: Odd adaptations | Includes index.
Identifiers: ISBN 9781538204054 (pbk.) | ISBN 9781538204078 (library bound) | ISBN 9781538204061 (6 pack)
Subjects: LCSH: Agamidae–Juvenile literature. | Lizards–Australia–Juvenile literature.Adaptation (Biology)–Juvenile literature.
Classification: LCC QL666.L223 F54 2018 | DDC 597.95'5–dc23

First Edition

Published in 2018 by
Gareth Stevens Publishing
111 East 14th Street, Suite 349
New York, NY 10003

Designer: Sarah Liddell
Editor: Kristen Nelson

Photo credits: Cover, p. 1 Marc Witte/Shutterstock.com; background used throughout Captblack76/Shutterstock.com; p. 4 Materialscientist/Wikimedia Commons; p. 5 defpicture/Shutterstock.com; p. 6 Chris Watson/Shutterstock.com; p. 7 Australian Scenics/Getty Images; p. 8 Tongsai/Shutterstock.com; p. 9 EcoPrint/Shutterstock.com; p. 10 Eric Isselee/Shutterstock.com; p. 11 Juliann/Shutterstock.com; p. 13 Svetlana Turchenick/Shutterstock.com; p. 14 Michiel de Wit/Shutterstock.com; p. 15 Photography by Mangiwau/Getty Images; p. 16 Fred the Oyster/Wikimedia Commons; p. 17 Kristian Bell/Shutterstock.com; p. 18 KeresH~commonswiki/Wikimedia Commons; p. 19 Ross Gordon Henry/Shutterstock.com; p. 21 Luke Wait/Shutterstock.com; p. 22 Tigerhawkvok/Wikimedia Commons; p. 23 Steve Shoup/Shutterstock.com; p. 24 Matt Jeppson/Shutterstock.com; p. 25 (sidewinder) Wdwdbot/Wikimedia Commons; p. 25 (fringe-toed lizard) pixy/Shutterstock.com; p. 26 bluedog studio/Shutterstock.com; p. 27 Benny Trapp/Wikimedia Commons; p. 28 dioch/Shutterstock.com; p. 29 The Sydney Morning Herald/Contributor/Fairfax Media/Getty Images.

Printed in China

CPSIA compliance information: Batch #CS17GS: For further information contact Gareth Stevens, New York, New York at 1-800-542-2595.

CONTENTS

Recognizing Reptiles 4

Head Trick 6

Bare Those Teeth 8

Hidden in Plain Sight 12

Strange Senses 16

Sand, Sun...and Adaptations! 20

All About Babies 26

Glossary 30

For More Information 31

Index 32

Words in the glossary appear in **bold** type the first time they are used in the text.

RECOGNIZING REPTILES

What is ectothermic and has scaly skin, a backbone, and lungs? Reptiles! **THIS ANIMAL GROUP INCLUDES TURTLES AND TORTOISES, LIZARDS AND SNAKES, CROCODILES AND ALLIGATORS, AND THE TUATARA.** Reptiles can be very different from one another. Some have legs, and some don't. Reptiles can be huge, like the saltwater crocodile, which can be up to 23 feet (7 m) long. Or they can be tiny, like the Jaragua lizard, which is about 1.2 inches (3 cm) long!

Reptiles have some of the coolest—and weirdest—adaptations in all the animal kingdom. From "tasting" the air to a third eye, these adaptations are almost unbelievable!

COOL TO BE COLD

An animal that's ectothermic is cold-blooded. Its body temperature depends on the temperature of its surroundings. **REPTILES ARE COLD-BLOODED AND NEED TO SPEND TIME IN THE SUN TO WARM UP. WHEN IT'S TOO HOT, THEY NEED TO HEAD TO THE SHADE OR UNDERGROUND TO COOL DOWN.**

JARAGUA LIZARD

ADAPTATIONS ARE LONG-TERM CHANGES IN ANIMALS' BODIES OR BEHAVIOR THAT MAKE THEM BETTER ABLE TO SURVIVE IN THEIR **ENVIRONMENT.** HERE, A CROCODILE LIES IN A SUNNY SPOT IN A RIVER TO WARM UP.

5

HEAD TRICK

Thorny devils are spiky lizards native to Australia that look just like their name suggests—they're covered in thorns! These spikes are an adaptation meant to keep predators from trying to eat them for lunch.

A SPIKY BUMP ON THE BACK OF A THORNY DEVIL'S NECK HAS AN EVEN MORE IMPORTANT PURPOSE. IT'S USED AS A SECOND HEAD! If they're scared, these lizards can tuck their real head between their front legs. Now, the big bump on their neck looks like their head! This can confuse predators and keep the thorny devil's head safe. What a cool adaptation!

THORNY DEVILS DUCK AND HIDE TO SHOW THEIR SECOND HEAD IF A PREDATOR IS NEAR!

SECOND HEAD

PROTECT YOURSELF!

Thorny devils have other ways to protect themselves from predators. First, they can fill their chest with air to look bigger. They also walk in an odd, slow, shaky way. They stop often. It's thought moving this way helps them hide from predators on the lookout for moving prey.

BARE THOSE TEETH

GECKOS ARE BORN WITH A FULL SET OF TEETH! Their cone-shaped teeth are specially adapted to help geckos survive, including when they sense danger. Most of the time, geckos are peaceful reptiles. But they'll bite people, predators, and even other geckos if they feel **threatened**. They use their teeth to fight for territory and mates, too.

Snakes also use their teeth to protect themselves. Some snakes have long, sharp teeth called fangs. All snakes lose and regrow teeth throughout their life. **THE PUFF ADDER MAY HAVE AS MANY AS SIX NEW FANGS DEVELOPING AT A TIME, JUST WAITING FOR AN OLD ONE TO FALL OUT!**

GECKO

NOTHING BUT THE TOOTH

Geckos' teeth have developed to be perfect for gecko meals—but they aren't used for chewing! Their teeth are used to catch and crush the bugs they like to eat. The teeth on the top and bottom of their jaw don't line up perfectly in order to do this well.

8

SNAKES, SUCH AS THIS PUFF ADDER, AREN'T THE ONLY REPTILES TO LOSE AND REGROW TEETH. MOST REPTILES DO THIS, INCLUDING GECKOS!

Snake fangs may be hollow or have channels, or grooves, in them. Poison called venom that snakes make in their body flows through their fangs or down the grooves when they bite. Venom is used when catching prey, but it's also an adaptation that helps snakes protect themselves.

THE KING COBRA CAN KILL AN ADULT ASIAN ELEPHANT IN A FEW HOURS IF IT BITES IN THE RIGHT PLACE! It's the world's longest venomous snake, growing

MORE THAN SNAKES

Lizards can be venomous, too! Gila monsters are the largest lizards in the United States. They have a strong bite, and many of their teeth have two grooves venom flows through as they bite! The Mexican beaded lizard, green iguana, and common water monitor also make venom, though iguana venom is very weak.

VENOMOUS SNAKES

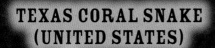

TEXAS CORAL SNAKE
(UNITED STATES)

EASTERN DIAMONDBACK
(UNITED STATES)

KING COBRA
(ASIA)

CHINESE COBRA
(CHINA)

BOOMSLANG
(AFRICA)

JARCARA
(BRAZIL)

GABOON VIPER
(AFRICA)

INLAND TAIPAN
(AUSTRALIA)

TERCIOPELO
(CENTRAL AMERICA)

KING BROWN SNAKE
(AUSTRALIA)

**THERE ARE VENOMOUS SNAKES FOUND
ALL OVER THE WORLD! THE INLAND TAIPAN
HAS THE WORLD'S DEADLIEST VENOM.**

HIDDEN IN PLAIN SIGHT

In order to hide from predators, many reptiles' coloring blends in to their surroundings. This is called camouflage. Bearded dragons take blending in one step further. **NOT ONLY DO THEY MATCH THEIR ENVIRONMENT, BEARDED DRAGONS CAN STAY VERY, VERY STILL.** This adaptation helps them survive because predators watch for any kind of movement around them!

Chameleons—lizards known for their color-changing talent—don't only change color to hide, though some do. Some species of chameleon use this adaptation to show bright colors needed for **communication**. **CHAMELEON COLORS CAN SHOW FEAR AND ANGER OR BE USED TO SEND A MESSAGE TO POSSIBLE MATES.**

A LIZARD OF A DIFFERENT COLOR

Bearded dragons can also change color. Their color change doesn't seem to be for camouflage. **SCIENTISTS THINK THEY LIGHTEN OR DARKEN THE COLOR OF THEIR BACKS TO MANAGE BODY TEMPERATURE AND CHANGE THEIR CHEST AND "BEARD" COLOR TO COMMUNICATE WITH OTHER BEARDED DRAGONS!**

SOME KINDS OF CHAMELEONS CAN CHANGE TO VERY BRIGHT COLORS, OTHERS ARE DULLER GREENS AND BROWNS.

13

Many turtles and tortoises are colored browns and greens in order to blend in to their surroundings. A snapping turtle's shell is also camouflage! It may just look like a big rock to yummy fish the turtle is waiting to eat.

Turtle shells also seem like an adaptation for protection. While shells do protect the turtle, some scientists don't think that's the reason turtles first developed them. **FOSSILS SHOW THAT MODERN TURTLES' SHELLS EVOLVED FROM THEIR ANCESTORS' RIBS!** Scientists think turtle ancestors needed to be better diggers, and wider ribs made their front legs stronger for digging. This adaptation would have made them great swimmers, too!

RIBS TO SHELL?

The change from ribs to shell took a very long time, like many adaptations do. First, turtle ancestors' lower ribs widened. Then, they fused and formed the lower shell. The same thing happened to the upper ribs and spine to form the top of the shell, or carapace.

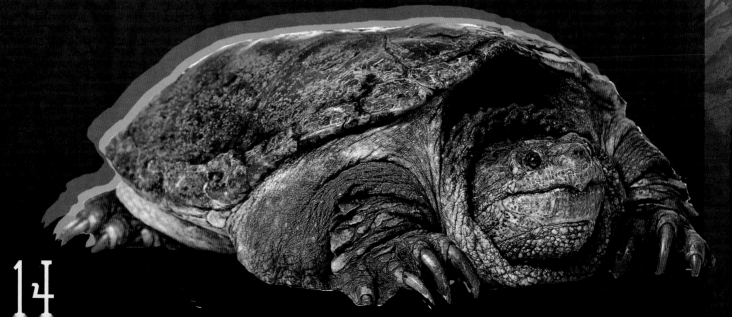

THESE SAW-SHELLED SNAPPING TURTLES CLEARLY BLEND IN TO THEIR WET ENVIRONMENT.

15

STRANGE SENSES

You use your nostrils, or the holes in your nose, to smell and breathe. Snakes have nostrils, too, but they're more important for breathing than smelling. **SNAKES USE THEIR TONGUE AND A SPECIAL ORGAN, OR BODY PART, ON THE ROOF OF THEIR MOUTH TO SMELL!** This Jacobson's organ is made of sensing cells and has two pits in it that perfectly fit the Y shape of a snake's tongue!

A snake flicks its tongue out of its mouth to gather odor **particles**. These particles are carried up to the Jacobson's organ. The chemicals they're made of send a message to the snake's brain. The smell is then identified!

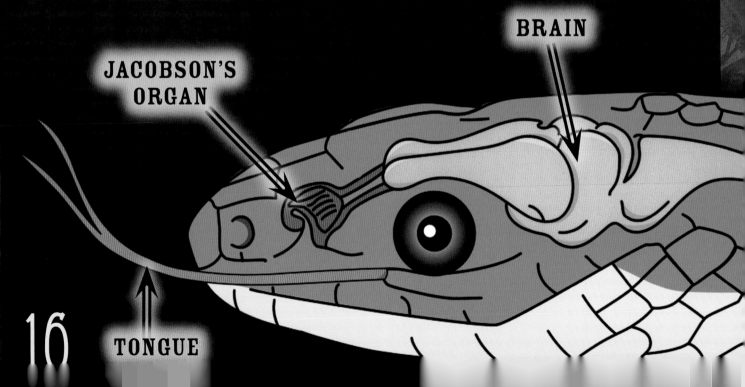

BRAIN

JACOBSON'S ORGAN

TONGUE

ON THE HUNT

Snakes use their Jacobson's organ mostly when they're hunting prey. The chemicals they pick up from the air with their tongue tell them what kind of prey they're hunting and also where the prey is!

SNAKES ARE THE BEST KNOWN FOR THIS ADAPTATION. HOWEVER, OTHER REPTILES, INCLUDING LIZARDS SUCH AS GILA MONSTERS AND GECKOS, USE THEIR TONGUE AND JACOBSON'S ORGAN TO "TASTE" THE AIR AROUND THEM.

Tuataras look a lot like lizards. However, these mysterious reptiles have a number of odd adaptations that set them apart. One of the strangest tuatara adaptations is their third eye! You can only see a tuatara's third eye if it's still very young. Scales grow over it a few months after birth.

STRANGELY, THOUGH THE TUATARAS' THIRD EYE HAS A RETINA, LENS, CORNEA, AND NERVE ENDINGS, WHICH ARE ALSO THE PARTS OF A REGULAR EYE, THIS THIRD EYE ISN'T USED FOR SEEING. It's found on top of their head and likely helps them tell the time of day or year.

TUATARA TEETH

Unlike other reptiles, tuataras don't grow new teeth if they're lost or as they wear down. These reptiles also have a special arrangement of teeth: two rows on top and one on the bottom. That's unlike any other reptile, too!

TUATARAS AREN'T THE ONLY ANIMALS THAT HAVE A THIRD EYE, CALLED A PARIETAL (PUH-RY-UH-TUHL) EYE. MANY TYPES OF LIZARDS, AS WELL AS SOME FROGS AND FISH, HAVE THIS STRANGE ADAPTATION.

TOTALLY ODD TUATARAS

TUATARAS HAVE A DOUBLE ROW OF TEETH ON THEIR UPPER JAW AND A SINGLE ROW ON THEIR LOWER JAW.

MALE TUATARAS CAN MAKE THEIR SPINES LOOK LIKE A FAN TO ATTRACT FEMALES.

TUATARAS LIKELY USE THEIR PARIETAL EYE TO TELL THE TIME OF DAY.

TUATARAS SHED, OR LOSE, THEIR SKIN ONCE A YEAR.

TUATARAS CAN LET THEIR TAILS FALL OFF AND THEN REGROW THEM.

SAND, SUN...AND ADAPTATIONS!

Because reptiles are cold-blooded, desert temperatures can be much too hot for them. Some reptiles adapt to the **extreme** daytime heat by being nocturnal, or mostly active at night. HOWEVER, SOME DESERT REPTILES CAN HANDLE THEIR BODY GETTING QUITE HOT. THE DESERT IGUANA IS ACTIVE WHEN ITS BODY IS 100°F TO 108°F (38°C TO 42°C)!

Desert reptiles have other behaviors to keep cool when it's hot during the day. THE NAMAQUA CHAMELEON CHANGES COLORS TO KEEP ITS TEMPERATURE IN CHECK! These lizards are almost black in the morning when it's cooler to take in heat from the sun. Later in the day, they're a lighter gray to reflect the light.

NOT TOO COLD

Reptiles have adapted to **habitats** all over the world, including near rivers, in deserts, and even forests. They commonly live near water and many spend a lot of time in it. REPTILES MOSTLY LIVE IN **TROPICAL** AND **TEMPERATE** CLIMATES. THEY DON'T OFTEN LIVE IN VERY COLD PLACES SUCH AS THE **TUNDRA**!

20

LIKE MANY DESERT REPTILES, DESERT CHAMELEONS LIKE THIS ONE ALSO DIG HOLES TO HIDE IN WHEN THEY NEED TO COOL DOWN.

21

THE DESERT TORTOISE SPENDS ABOUT 95 PERCENT OF ITS LIFE IN UNDERGROUND BURROWS. It lives in the Sonoran Desert in southwestern North America where the temperature can rise to almost 120°F (49°C). In order to survive, desert tortoises dig holes all over their habitat to hide in.

When it's hottest in the summer, desert tortoises go into estivation, or a period of inactivity during hot and dry times. Their **bladder** is specially adapted to these long periods where they may drink very little. **A DESERT TORTOISE'S BLADDER CAN HOLD AS MUCH AS 40 PERCENT OF ITS WEIGHT IN WATER AND WASTES**

DESERT TORTOISE

THE BIG SLEEP

Many desert animals are inactive for long periods when the weather isn't ideal for their survival. They burrow into the ground and come out when temperatures are higher or lower. Leopard lizards are only active in the desert when the temperature is over 80°F (27°C). They're inactive for about 8 months of the year!

Walking on sand is hard! Desert reptiles have adapted to move well through or over sand in their habitat. **THE FRINGE-TOED LIZARD HAS AN ADAPTATION THAT ALLOWS IT TO RUN ON SAND!** The long toes of its back feet have pointed scales that give it **traction** as it moves across the sandy desert.

Legless lizards and some desert snakes, such as the banded sand snake, are said to "swim" through sand. They have small heads and eyes and smooth scales that let them move through sand like other animals swim through water! What's more, they can breathe through the sand as they move!

LEGLESS LIZARDS LIKE THIS ONE HAVE ADAPTED TO MOVEMENT IN THEIR ENVIRONMENTS BY EVOLVING AWAY FROM HAVING LEGS FOR WALKING!

The sidewinder, a snake that's a kind of pit viper, doesn't slither like most other snakes because of its hot, sandy home. The sidewinder only allows two points on its body to touch the ground at a time! That's one way to stay cool!

FRINGE-TOED LIZARD

ALL ABOUT BABIES

Most kinds of reptiles lay many eggs. The shells are often soft and leathery, but some can be hard. Other reptiles give birth to live young, including about 20 percent of lizards and snakes.

ONE LIZARD, THE YELLOW-BELLIED THREE-TOED SKINK, IS CHANGING FROM EGG LAYING TO LIVE BIRTH RIGHT NOW! Scientists have found that these skinks lay eggs when they live on the coast. When they live in the mountains, however, they've started having live babies. This may be because the skink moms living in the mountains need to protect their babies inside their body longer. That's adaptation in action!

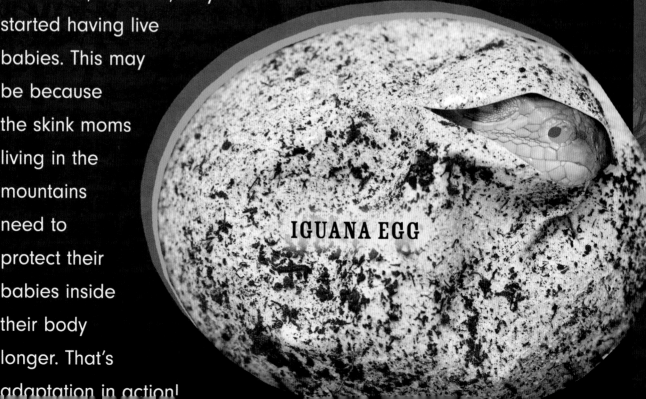

IGUANA EGG

STRANGE SKINKS

Skinks are a kind of lizard that often burrow. Those that dig underground have a see-through "window" scale that protects their eyes as they move through the earth. Some burrowing skinks have fewer legs or eardrums found very deep in their heads. All these adaptations help them survive!

SKINKS ARE FOUND ALL OVER THE WORLD, INCLUDING IN SOUTHEAST ASIA, AUSTRALIA, AND TEMPERATE PARTS OF NORTH AMERICA.

Keeping babies safe is the reason for many behavioral adaptations in reptiles. Eggs and young need to be protected in order for a species to survive!

Mother crocodiles bury 35 to 50 eggs in a nest made in the loose dirt near water. For 2 to 3 months, the crocodile mom guards her eggs hidden in the nest.

When the baby crocodiles are ready to come out, they start making a chirping noise. **THE MOTHER DIGS UP HER BABIES AND CARRIES THEM TO THE WATER IN HER MOUTH!** While crocodiles do have big teeth, the mother carries as many as 15 babies very carefully.

STAYING CLOSE TO MOM

After the crocodile mother carries her babies to the water, she abandons them. Alligator babies, on the other hand, stay with their mother for as long as 2 years! Baby alligators have to survive many predators, including birds, bobcats, and sometimes other alligators.

BABY CROCODILE

LIKE CROCODILES, MOTHER
ALLIGATORS (SHOWN HERE)
PROTECT THEIR NEST OF EGGS.

GLOSSARY

bladder: a stretchable body part that stores liquid waste until it can be removed from the body

burrow: a hole made by an animal in which it lives or hides. Also, to dig the hole.

communication: the sharing of thoughts or feelings by sound, movement, or writing

develop: to grow and change

environment: the conditions that surround a living thing and affect the way it lives

evolve: to grow and change over time

extreme: to a very great degree

habitat: the natural place where an animal or plant lives

inject: to use sharp teeth to force venom into an animal's body

particle: a very small piece of something

temperate: mild climate that's not too hot or too cold

threatened: in danger

traction: the stickiness between two surfaces, such as feet and the ground

tropical: having to do with the warm parts of Earth near the equator

tundra: cold northern lands that lack forests and have permanently frozen soil below the surface

FOR MORE INFORMATION

BOOKS

Gray, Leon. *Amazing Animal Shape-Shifters*. North Mankato, MN: Capstone Press, 2016.

Hirschmann, Kris. *Deadliest Reptiles*. San Diego, CA: ReferencePoint Press, Inc., 2016.

Riehecky, Janet. *Reptiles*. North Mankato, MN: Capstone Press, 2014.

WEBSITES

Animal Adaptations
ecokids.ca/swf-files/gamesPage/adaptations.swf
Match animal adaptations to the correct animal in this game!

Reptiles
kids.nationalgeographic.com/animals/hubs/reptiles/
Read about all different kinds of reptiles on this website.

INDEX

babies 26, 28

camouflage 12, 14 ,15

cold-blooded 4, 20

color change 12, 13, 20

communication 12

dig holes 21, 22, 27

eggs 26, 28, 29

estivation 22

fangs 8, 10

habitat 20, 22, 24

Jacobson's organ 16, 17

legless lizards 24

live young 26

mates 8, 12

move through sand 24, 25

nocturnal 20

second head 6

shell 14

spikes 6

teeth 8, 9, 10, 18, 28

third eye 4, 18

venom 10, 11